MW01483920

FOR EVERYDAY LIFE

Dr. Felisha Ford

EDITION ONE
Pearls
FOR EVERYDAY LIFE

Copyright © 2018 by Dr. Felisha Ford

To order products, or for any other correspondence:

Dr. Felisha Ford
PO Box 311472
Enterprise, Alabama 36331
www.drfelishaford.com

ISBN-13:978-1541275997

ISBN-10:1541275993

Dedication

I would like to dedicate *Pearls for Everyday Life* to every woman who strives to live a life of purity, peace, and wholeness through the wisdom given to us through the Word of God. Your desire to please God and adorn yourself with the beauty of holiness is going to produce goodness in your life in every way!

I also affectionately dedicate this book to my loving family, especially my dear husband and high school sweetheart, Bishop Demetrius Ford. You all are the sweetness of my life, and my daily inspiration to grow and develop into everything God created me to be. I would not know love or life the way I do were it not for you all in my life.

Acknowledgements

This book could not have been completed without the faithful support of my husband, Bishop Demetrius Ford, who has always inspired me to grow in my faith and realize my maximum potential. I am also grateful for my two sons – Demetrius "Dejuan" II and Josiyah – who kindly gave me the space and time to write this book without complaint. Without your patience, love, and stories, I would not have finished. Of course, I cannot thank my parents enough – James and Shelia Talley – for their constant encouragement and prayers. Thank you also to my siblings, who are always there for me and support me more than they know.

A special thanks to Tierra, my daughter-by-love, for investing her time, skill, and creativity in assisting me with the entire publishing process from start to finish. You are God's gift to me! I am also grateful to my church family for their love and prayerful support.

I would also like to acknowledge the exceptional work of my editor, Elisabeth Alexander. Thank you for working diligently and thoroughly to help me publish high-quality work.

Above all, I acknowledge the endless love and power given to me by God to fulfill the destiny He appointed me. I am nothing and can do nothing, without Him.

PEARLS

Pearls
FOR EVERYDAY LIFE

Pearl 1
Expect the Great

You are walking into a season of open doors and great opportunities! Don't settle for doing what you've always done and being what you've always been. God is releasing fresh oil and is breathing a refreshing wind that will cause you to become dissatisfied with "average" and status quo and elevate your level of expectancy and progress. No matter the opposition; no matter the hard work it will require; no matter how the stumbling blocks and insecurities may try to hinder your pursuit for greater - keep watching for divine opportunities. Believe God to take you higher in every area of your life in your new season of greatness! The divine power that is within you is greater than any opposing force coming against you. Expect the great! Focus on the open door, not the opposition,

or you will miss the opportunity!

For a great and effective door has opened to me,

and there are many adversaries.

(I Corinthians 16:9 NKJV)

Today's Declaration:

I am expecting and pursuing greater in my life!

Pearl 2
Be Faithful

Faithfulness is a choice. When you are faithful to God in your service and obedience to Him, it makes God smile! Faithfulness that has to be forced or coerced displeases God. Rather, faithfulness should be rooted in your love for Him. God has lovingly given you a free will; you choose whether or not to be faithful. When you choose obedience over disobedience, righteousness over sin, faith over fear, kingdom building over idleness, submission over selfishness, or praise over complaining, you bring God joy. By doing this, you are demonstrating your allegiance and love to Him through your faithfulness. The more faithful you are in the small things that God requires of you and gives

4

you to do, the more trustworthy you become to Him. The more trustworthy you become, the more God will bless you and trust you with more. So, in everything, choose faithfulness!

I have chosen to be faithful; I have determined to live by your regulations. (Psalm 119:30 NLT)

Today's Declaration:

I choose to be faithful in everything God has chosen me to do!

Pearl 3
Resist Fear

Fear is a hindering spirit that stifles change, growth, and progression in the lives of those who give it power to do so. Fear can be described as a distressing emotion produced by the belief of impending danger, evil, or pain - whether the threat is real or imagined. Most of your fears are false imaginations sent by the devil to cause you to worry and fear things that God never planned to happen. But the perfect love that God has for you casts out all fear, and He replaces fear with spiritual virtues that give you power to conquer it! Resist fear by walking in God's power, love, and soundness of mind, and the spirit of fear *must* flee from you.

For God has not given us the spirit of fear, but of

power and of love and of a sound mind.

(II Tim. 1:7 NKJV)

Today's Declaration:

Fear no longer has control over me!

Pearl 4
Ask for the Big

My family and I went to a very popular family
entertainment venue with games and prizes once,
and the Lord taught me an amazing lesson while
there! When my young sons went to cash in their
tokens for toys, they were saddened when they
discovered they did not have enough tokens for the
prizes they wanted. A lady who was watching what
was going on came up to us and asked us, "What
do the boys want?" Not wanting to ask for too
much, I chose a reasonably ticketed toy. She asked
me again, "What do the boys want?" I told her
what I knew the boys wanted, knowing the toy was
a high-ticket item. To my shock and surprise, this
kind lady had won the jackpot and could buy

anything in the store! God used this moment,

showing me that many of us miss out on valuable

blessings because we do not believe God enough to

ask him for the true desires of our hearts,

believing they are "too much" or "too big" to ask of

Him. Ask God for the *big*! His supply is endless;

the whole earth and everything in it belongs to

Him!

"If you then, being evil, know how to give good gifts

to your children, how much more will your Father

who is in heaven give what is good to those who

ask Him!" (Matthew 7:11 NKJV)

Today's Declaration:

I will not be afraid to ask God to do greater and

bigger things in my life!

Pearl 5
Rejoice in Victory

"Victory is mine!" These are the words of rejoicing that should be on your lips when you are facing hardship and trials. Even when it seems as if trouble is perpetually coming after you on every side, you will not be destroyed or harmed in the midst of it if you run into the presence of your Almighty God who is your strongtower! His presence will calm and strengthen you, and His Spirit will protect you against the floods of trouble and difficulty that try to overwhelm you. Take a deep breath, run to the safety that lies in God, and rest in His hiding place with the praises of victory on your lips. Neither the devil nor the trouble he brings will be able to touch you there. The devil cannot pluck you out of God's hands. You are safe!

You are my hiding place; you protect me from

trouble. You surround me with songs of victory.

(Psalm 32:7 NLT)

Today's Declaration:

No matter the trouble, my heart will rejoice in

divine victory!

Pearl 6
Freedom from Struggles

Debilitating cycles. Destructive habits. Faulty

thinking. Struggles with sin. Many ask, "How can I

break free?" Jesus overcame, and He has given

you power to overcome! Jesus came to break the

trap of bondage and sin in the lives of those who

believe in Him. He came in the flesh and was

tempted in every manner in which you are being

tempted yet He remained without sin. Therefore,

He understands the battle that wages in your mind

between what your spirit and flesh desire. But,

there is a greater power available to you than your

sheer willpower, positive thinking, or personal

resolve that will perpetuate everlasting freedom in

your life; that almighty power is only found in His

cleansing blood! If you call on Jesus' name with a

repentant heart, you will be delivered! The question

is, "do you truly desire to be free?"

Oh, what a miserable person I am! Who will free me

from this life that is dominated by sin and death?

Thank God! The answer is in Jesus Christ our Lord.

(Romans 7:24-25 NLT)

Today's Declaration:

I am free from the struggles of my past, present,

and future through Jesus Christ!

Pearl 7
Show Me the Right Way

There is a way that seems right to a man, but its end is the way of death. (Prov. 14:12). In these times, the spirits of deception and confusion are running rampant. Therefore, you must be careful to exercise spiritual discernment in the decisions that you make in every area of your life. You will be tempted to indulge and fall prey to things and relationships that come in seducing packages that promise increased security and fulfillment, and because it may be appealing to the flesh, many will deceive themselves into thinking it has been approved by God. But, you must be careful not to place your own wisdom above the Lord's wisdom. Quiet your soul - your mind, will, and emotions -

and listen for God's voice and instructions. He will show you the right path to take that will lead to life and peace. God's plans for your life are right and good, and they will produce a prosperous end!

Keep me from lying to myself; give me the privilege of knowing your instructions. (Psalm 119:29 NLT)

Today's Declaration:

I will walk in the paths of righteousness that lead to life and peace!

PEARL 8
Have Fun

While cleaning my house one day, my 8-year old son said, "Mom, you need to have more fun." Not really knowing how to respond, I began to ponder on his statement and the truth of it. Because of the many "hats" we wear and responsibilities we have, it is incredibly easy to get lost in the grind of a busy life and hectic daily schedule. We are often so wrapped up that we do not take out the time to just simply have fun. A merry heart does good, like medicine (Prov. 17:22). Happiness and joy are natural stimulants, and relaxation replenishes the mind and body. So, I encourage you to take this journey with me. Learn to make time for the fun we can have in our daily lives! You only have one life to live; live it to the fullest!

So I recommend having fun, because there is nothing better for people in this world than to eat, drink, and enjoy life. That way they will experience some happiness along with all the hard work God gives them under the sun. (Ecclesiastes 8:15 NLT)

Today's Declaration:

I will make time for more fun in my life!

PEARL 9
Wait for Instruction

I was teaching a psychology class, and a test was coming up the next class session. I gave the students the study guide for the test at the beginning of class. Big mistake! After I gave them the study guide, which was just an empty shell of what was needed to pass the test, they quickly developed "false confidence" certain they could pass the test with only the study guide. Some of them, burning with "spring fever," left the class before the full instructions were given on how to successfully pass the test. Their test grades reflected their decisions, and several regretted their choice to have hurried along before fully understanding their instructions. Be careful not to run off with only a glimpse or partial instruction

18

on what is needed to pass life's tests. Choose to sit still long enough to receive the detailed instructions from the omniscient God who knows exactly what will be required of you during your next test and what wisdom you will need to succeed in it. Zeal without knowledge oftentimes produces failure, but embracing wisdom and instruction can lead to great success!

Get all the advice and instruction you can, so you will be wise the rest of your life.

(Proverbs 19:20 NLT)

Today's Declaration:

I will quiet my soul and wait on God's instructions for my situations.

19

PEARL 10
Living Carefree

Wouldn't it be wonderful to live a carefree life? Well, guess what? That is God's will for your life! His desire is that when trouble arises, your heart does not become overwhelmed or anxious and your mind does not become worried or confused. Rather, in the face of trouble and bad circumstances, His will is for you to rejoice. He wants you to lay down your weights and burdens before Him, to fix your thoughts on good things and the truth of His word, and to completely trust him to deliver you out of every circumstance. It is God's desire for you to cast all of your cares upon him because He cares for you. He wants you to be carefree (free of care) not careful (full of care).

So, if you really want to be carefree, the choice is yours. Choose to be carefree!

Be careful f or nothing; but in everything by prayer and supplication with thanksgiving let your requests be made known unto God. (Phil. 4:6 KJV)

Today's Declaration:

I choose to live a carefree life by casting all of my cares on God!

Pearl 11
Guaranteed Victory

"God is saying 'guaranteed victory' for those who believe and will praise Him in advance for turning it around!" My Pastor declared those words so powerfully and prophetically one Sunday. When he spoke the words "guaranteed victory," great anticipation literally leaped within my spirit, and my faith revived and grew to a whole different level at that moment! Immediately, I saw victory, I felt victory, and I declared victory with nothing wavering, even in the situations in my life where there had been uncertainty, doubt, and fear. So, I speak the same empowering words over your life: guaranteed victory! No ifs, ands, or buts about it. No matter how bad it looks, feels, or seems. Victory is yours today, and failure is not an option. God says, "guaranteed victory!"

God is not a man, that He should lie, nor a son of man, that He should repent. Has He said, and will He not do? Or has He spoken, and will He not make it good? (Numbers 23:19 NKJV)

Today's Declaration:

I decree "guaranteed victory" in every trial and situation I encounter in my life.

Pearl 12
God Never Changes

In a world where everything and everyone seems to change day by day, it is refreshing to know that God is a constant and never-changing presence in our lives. His love is unfailing. His mercies are new every morning. His provision is manifested daily. His redemption is everlasting. He *never* changes! He is *always* dependable, *always* loving, *always* just, *always* comforting, and he is *always* there no matter what the circumstance or situation. God has promised us that He will be with us *always* and *never* leave us. Whatever He has promised us, He will certainly make it good. He has promised us that whatever gifts He has given to us to bring His name glory, they are irrevocable. He will not change His mind concerning us. God is with us on the mountaintops, but He is also with us in the

valleys, the floods, and in the fires of life. God is

always there, and He *never* changes!

I am the Lord, and I do not change. (Malachi 3:6)

Today's Declaration:

I put my complete trust in my God who never

changes!

Pearl 13
Jesus Over You

My husband describes the acronym J.O.Y. as

JESUS OVER YOU! When you are experiencing

disappointments, remember to place Jesus over

you! Allow Jesus to reign over your troubled mind,

your negative circumstances, and your

weaknesses and fears. He promises to fill your

heart with unspeakable joy which will give you

strength to endure and to rejoice in the face of trial

and hardship! Joy can only be realized when we

walk in the power of the Holy Spirit and when we

allow the fruit of joy to be developed in us. We

have to choose to rejoice over complaining and to

focus on what is going well over what may be going

wrong realizing that true joy is untouched by our

circumstances. Joy is a constant feeling ofcomfort

and contentment regardless of the state we are in.
A joyful heart believes that "Jesus is over me," and
He will allow nothing to happen to you that He has
not already fully equipped you for and given you
the victory.

But let all those rejoice who put their trust in You;

let them ever shout for joy, because You defend

them; let those also who love Your name be joyful in

You. (Psalm 5:11 NKJV)

Today's Declaration:

"Jesus is over me!" Therefore, I will rejoice and
have joy every day and in every circumstance!

Pearl 14
Amazing Grace

Thank God for his amazing grace! As you are striving to reach the mark that God has set before you, sometimes you may falter along the way. It is in those times that you may be tempted to give up, to quit or to remain in that fallen state because of the shame, guilt, and discouragement. But good news! All is not lost! God's amazing grace - his undeserved love and favor - is extended to those of a repentant and broken heart! God's amazing grace will lift you up, clean you up, and give you a fresh start. So, get up, and get back in the race! It's not over! God has given you amazing grace for the amazing race! If you confess your sins to God, His grace, faithfulness, and forgiveness will be made available to you to cleanse you from all unrighteousness (1 John 1:9). God embraces those of a repentant heart and mind, and He will restore, strengthen, and redirect your footsteps towards the path He has set for you. That is the phenomenal power of God's amazing grace!

For though the righteous fall seven times, they rise again. (Proverbs 24:16a NIV)

Today's Declaration:

I thank God for His amazing grace that keeps me day by day!

Pearl 15
God Has Chosen You

Imperfections. Struggles. Insecurities. Disabilities. Anxieties. In spite of, God still chooses you! God still wants to use you. God still wants to bless you. God still wants to favor you. God still wants to be close to you. Nothing that we do, experience, or suffer with can separate you from God's love or change the destiny He has planned for your life. It is He who called you, chose you, justified you, and glorified you. When you feel you have been counted out, God still says, "I choose you!" And, not only has God chosen you, but He has already planned for you to do amazing things that will produce greatness in you and in the people and world around you. He chose you not because you were perfect, but because you are imperfect which ensures that you will seek Him for strength in your areas of weakness. God loves being your strength and empowering you to do what you know you could never do in your own power!

You did not choose Me, but I chose you and appointed you that you should go and bear fruit, and that your fruit should remain, that whatever you ask the Father in My name He may give you.
(John 15:16 NKJV)

Today's Declaration:

God has chosen me for greatness!

Pearl 16
The Lord Is Calling

Prayer and meditation; times of fasting and spiritual purification; quietness and stillness before the Lord; how do you respond when you hear the Lord calling you to submit yourself and commit your time to priceless opportunities to fellowship, commune, and receive from His treasures of wisdom, strength, or revelation? Many are too busy seeking these from other sources, or are operating in a spirit of self-sufficiency rather than seeking the One who is the source of them all. God promises us, if you draw close to Him, He will draw close to you; and if you seek His face, you will find Him (James 4:8; Jer. 29:13). Desire Him above all else, and answer Him with your heart when He calls for sacred time with you. He will fill your heart with good things until it overflows! If you answer God's call for greater intimacy with Him, you will experience Him in a way unimaginable and deeper than you ever have before.

My heart has heard you say, "Come and talk to Me," and my heart responds, "Lord, I'm coming."

(Psalm 27:8 NLT)

Today's Declaration:

Lord, I am answering the call for deeper intimacy with you!

Pearl 17
At a Crossroad

Not sure what to do at this point in your life? Not
clear on what direction to take? All of us have
experienced crossroads in life. We know we can't
stay stuck where we are because we feel God
compelling us to shift directions and travel a
different, more fulfilling path. Oftentimes, you find
yourself confused because there are so many
paths before you. Which do you take? How can
you be certain? In these times, who can you trust
to show you the right way to go? Trust the God
who created you! Trust the One who uniquely
designed you to travel the paths that will take you
to your divine purpose and expected end. Seek
God and learn to acknowledge Him in all of your
ways, and He promises to direct your paths!

Your ears shall hear a word behind you, saying,

"This is the way, walk in it," Whenever you turn to

the right hand or whenever you turn to the left.

(Isaiah 30:21 NKJV)

Today's Declaration:

I will follow only where the Lord leads me!

Pearl 18
You Have What It Takes

Do you know that God has gifted and anointed you to do a mighty work for Him? Your personality, your unique talents and abilities, and even your past struggles are all pieces of your life that God uses to increase the effectiveness of your spiritual gift and anointing. Sometimes the devil tries to use the very things that God desires to work for you to deter you from carrying out your Godly assignments. The enemy would have you to think your personality is too overbearing or too timid, that your past is too terrible, or your talents and abilities are not unique or special enough to be used by God. Well, guess what? God handcrafted you and handpicked you for your assignment, and He has already placed everything you need within you to excel at the work He has chosen you to do.

So, no more excuses; you have what it takes!

Take heed to the ministry which you have received

in the Lord, that you may fulfill it.

(Colossians 4:17 NKJV)

Today's Declaration:

I have what it takes to complete the assignment

God has given me!

Pearl 19
Power Lies Within You

Why are you waiting for someone to come and rescue you from the trouble you are in when God has anointed you with the power to get yourself out? Take a deep breath. Gird up your strength. Realize the divine power within you, and follow God's instruction that will lead you and those around you to victory and freedom! Gideon (in Judges 6) found himself surrounded by trouble, and his heart and mind were filled with thoughts of defeat, fear, inferiority, and insecurities. In the midst of his trouble, God sent an angel to reveal to Gideon that the power that was needed to deliver him and God's people was resting on the inside of him. He was the "mighty man of valor" that God wanted to use to bring deliverance (Judges 6:12)!

Could it be that you are overlooking your own strength? God has empowered *you* through His strength to deliver you from the situation and struggle you are in.

Then the Lord turned to him and said, "Go in this might of yours, and you shall save Israel from the hand of the Midianites. Have I not sent you?"

(Judges 6:14 NKJV)

Today's Declaration:

I am a mighty woman of valor full of courage and strength!

Pearl 20
Your Help Is Here

Today is your day! You have been praying and believing God for breakthroughs, deliverance, and miracles to take place in your life. You have been crying out to God and trusting Him to move in your life in some desperate situations. There were times when you thought God wasn't hearing your cry, and you felt abandoned and alone in your trouble. God has heard you when you cried out to Him, and He was there all of the time. God is your present help in your time of trouble, and your help is here! "According to your faith, be it unto you." (Matt. 9:29b) So, let your faith be revived and your hope be renewed that your help is here, and your wait is over! Today is your day!

For God says, "At just the right time, I heard you.

On the day of salvation, I helped you." Indeed, the

"right time" is now. Today is the day of salvation.

(II Cor. 6:2 NLT)

Today's Declaration:

I believe God is my Helper and that He is helping

me right now!

Pearl 21
Cast Your Cares

What are you constantly worrying about? What is causing you great anxiety, stress, and fear? From the smallest to the greatest details of your life, God is concerned about you. His will is for you to walk in peace and soundness of mind. So, He gives you the sweet and loving invitation to cast *everything* that is bothering and burdening you upon *Him* so you can enjoy His gift of peace. To "cast" in the Hebrew means "to throw with haste." In other words, as soon as you feel your heart or mind becoming gripped by trouble, fear, stress or anxiety, immediately give it to Jesus, and do not try to handle it in your own strength. Walk in peace!

Give all your worries and cares to God, for he cares

about you. (I Peter 5:7 NLT)

Today's Declaration:

I am casting all of my cares upon God, and I am

walking in peace!

Pearl 22
Let It Go

Forgetting the disappointments, failures, cycles, and issues of the past may be very difficult; but, let it go! God is giving you new life and is showing you a better way! Don't conform any longer to the old you, but embrace the fresh start God is giving you through the new you. God challenges you today to take off the old man and put on the new man that has been created after the likeness of God. A new mind, new ways, new vision, new desires, new destiny, and new perspectives await you. There is a much higher road God has destined you to travel as a "new man." So, get ready, get set, and go! Start your new journey to your new life and greater destiny without fear and without delay!

Behold, I will do a new thing, now it shall spring

forth; shall you not know it? (Isaiah 43:19a NKJV)

Today's Declaration:

I am letting go of the old and embracing the new,

in Jesus' Name!

Pearl 23
Don't Worry

Are you fretful or anxious about what tomorrow is going to bring in your life? The Lord is saying to you today to take no thought for tomorrow, but embrace the joys and handle the situations you are experiencing today in His grace and wisdom. God has already planned your tomorrows, and they are plans for good and not for disaster, to give you a future and a hope. Learn to rest in God today and trust with full assurance that God will take care of you today, tomorrow, and forevermore! No worries, no fears, no anxieties, no uncertainties – just faith in the omniscient and omnipresent God who already had every detail of your life planned out before a single day in your life passed. Walk in peace, and trust God with your future. You are in good hands!

My future is in Your hands. (Psalm 31:15a NLT)

Today's Declaration:

God, I trust you with my life!

Pearl 24
God Can Do Anything

Do you believe God can do anything? Do you

believe He can heal your body, save your family,

bless you financially, restore your soul, and quiet

your storm? Sometimes because of life's hard

knocks and disappointments, your faith in the God

you know can do the impossible becomes

weakened. You begin to lose hope, and your faith

begins to waiver the more difficult the problem

becomes for you. I want to encourage you to shake

off the weariness and weights of doubt, fear, and

discouragement and believe again! Trust again!

Have faith again! Ask again! What seems

impossible to man is possible with God! There is

nothing too hard for Him! When you believe and

ask in faith, in accordance to God's will, anything

can happen!

Yes, ask me for anything in My Name, and I will do

it! (John 14:14 NLT)

Today's Declaration:

I believe God can do anything!

Pearl 25
Pass It On

One time, my family and I went to a popular family
entertainment venue that has a large variety of
video games and food. A young man walked up to
us and offered us a gift card that contained
unlimited access to the race car games! My boys
were so excited, and I even partook in the fun and
games! I was so appreciative and inspired by his
random act of kindness that, when it was time to
leave, I sought out another family to bless with
this gift. How often do you take the time to show
random acts of kindness and love to others whom
you do not know? More importantly, how often do
you share with others the gift of Jesus Christ who
gives you unlimited access to His blessings?
Someone shared Jesus with you, and enabled the

change He brings to your life. Perpetuate this

unspeakable gift of the Good News of Jesus Christ,

by passing it on!

The fruit of the righteous is a tree of life, and he who

wins souls is wise. (Proverbs 11:30 NKJV)

Today's Declaration:

I will share Jesus with someone today!

Pearl 26
Pass the Test

What do you do when you go through trials?

During your seasons of struggle and suffering, you

may tend to grow weary and want to give up on

your dreams, desires, and faith. You become

frustrated and discouraged, and you want to stop

doing what is right. During those times of

vulnerability, the devil tries to blind your mind to

the truth that even in your season of suffering,

God is always with you, and He will never forsake

or fail you. It is also in those hard seasons that

God is testing you to see if you will continue to

walk in righteousness and trust Him in spite of it

all. So, don't give up in this season. Don't grow

weary in doing well. Endure and pass the test.

Seasons do change!

So if you are suffering in a manner that pleases God,

keep on doing what is right, and trust your lives to

the God who created you, for he will never fail you.

(I Peter 4:19 NLT)

Today's Declaration:

I will not get tired of doing what is right!

Pearl 27
Be Still

Sometimes when things are going awry in your life, you panic and busily begin trying to do everything in your power to try to fix it. You move so quickly into your "fixing mode" that you do not take adequate time to be still and seek God in quietness for His way and solution for your issues and circumstances. Often, you are too busy trying to "fix it," so intently that you drown out God's soft answer He whispers in the stillness and quietness that occur when you step back from the situation and sit still before Him. In your quiet times with God, when you hear His still, small voice, your finite wisdom becomes subservient to His infinite wisdom. Your will and desires become lost in His, as you wait for Him to move not by your power or strength, but by His Spirit. What if God says to you in the midst of the turmoil to just be still and trust Him? Would you obey?

Be still, and know that I am God. (Psalm 46:10 NLT)

Today's Declaration:

I will be still, and wait on God!

Pearl 28
It Is for God's Glory

My pastor declared one Sunday morning that every area the devil attacks in our lives is an area where God's glory is about to be revealed. What a powerful revelation! As I began to reflect on that statement, I thought about biblical testimonies like Daniel in the lions' den; the Hebrew boys in the fiery furnace; the Israelites at the Red Sea; Job losing it all; Lazarus' death; and Jesus being crucified. In every situation where the enemy attacked and thought he had won, God's glory - the true essence of His goodness and power - was revealed and delivered each of them in an unimaginably powerful way! Always remember: in times of spiritual attack and affliction, it is not about you. It is about God's glory being revealed through your life. Can God trust you to endure the

hardship so that He may be glorified?

Many are the afflictions of the righteous, but the

LORD delivers him out of them all.

(Psalm 34:19 NKJV)

Today's Declaration:

God will deliver me out of my affliction and get the

glory from my life!

Pearl 29
God is Up To Something

Are you going through tough times in your life right now that you just don't understand? Have you been blind-sided and sucker-punched with situations and issues that you did not even fathom would (or could) take place in your life? It hurts. It is disappointing, and it is frustrating. In the midst of what you're facing, are you willing to trust that God is still in control? That He is able to work out every situation for your good and sustain you while you are in your spiritual battle? God is going to cause great things to manifest about who you are and who He is through your trials. You do not have to understand what God is doing; just learn to trust Him! He is working on things behind the scenes for you that you could not imagine. So, be patient, and allow Him to see you through it all.

God is up to something great!

God thunders marvelously with His voice; He does

great things which we cannot comprehend.

(Job 37:5 NKJV)

Today's Declaration:

God is doing great things in my life!

Pearl 30
Love On Another Level

Loving family and friends is generally very easy to do, but what about showing the love of Christ to our enemies, to those who hurt us, or to those we may not know? It is easy to get caught in the love triangle of me, family, and friends and think we are doing well. But, the Bible says even sinners do that (Luke 6:32). The Lord's challenge to the believer is to love on another level which means loving our enemies, doing good and praying for those who spitefully use us, and revealing God's love to others even those outside of our love triangle. What expression of love can you offer to someone today who is outside of your love triangle? Offer a kind word, forgiveness, a smile, a prayer, a phone call. Be intentional, and love on God's level!

But I say to you, love your enemies, bless those who

curse you, do good to those who hate you, and pray

for those who spitefully use you and persecute you,

that you may be sons of your Father in heaven.

(Matt. 5:44-45a NKJV)

Today's Declaration:

I will love openly, unconditionally, and unselfishly!

Pearl 31
Hold On

What do you do when you are in trouble and you feel like God is not moving fast enough to rescue you? Do you get frustrated? Speak out of anger? Try to determine your own way out, or give up? A preacher gave a great illustration of what we should do in times of trouble by asking a question: when you are on an airplane and you experience turbulence, do you find an exit out of the plane and jump out immediately or do you begin to pray, buckle your seat belt, and hold on until it is over? So it is with the turbulence of life. There is no need to shout in anger against God, no need to try to immediately escape, no need to give up hope, just hold on in quiet assurance that the God, who allowed the trouble to come, will protect you in it and give you the victory!

Let all that I am wait quietly before God, for my hope is in him. My victory and honor come from God alone. He is my refuge, a rock where no enemy can reach me. (Psalm 62:5, 7 NLT)

Today's Declaration:

I will wait in quiet confidence for God's deliverance!

Pearl 32
Walk by Faith

Now faith is the substance of things hoped for, the evidence of things not seen (Hebrews 11:1). Walking by faith is not always easy to do. It challenges your intellect, natural senses, and is often in direct opposition to your emotions or feelings. But walking by faith also has many benefits that far outweigh its challenges. Walking by faith brings a peace that surpasses all human understanding. It births unspeakable joy and a life full of glory which pleases God and makes Him smile. It releases God's mighty hand to act in your favor, and produces results that exceed your loftiest expectations! Walking by faith is not easy, but it surely pays off! Will you walk by faith and enjoy its rewards?

For we walk by faith, and not by sight.

(2 Cor. 5:7 NKJV)

Today's Declaration:

I will walk by faith!

Pearl 33
The Grace to Forgive

Forgiving others who wronged or offended you can be very difficult. Trying to do this in the flesh causes the forgiver to feel weak, slighted, and entitled to some sort of continual restitution from the one forgiven. The attitude is "I may forgive, but I'll never forget!" But, forgiving through the Spirit of God causes the forgiver to extend grace and mercy freely with no expectation of restitution; the debt has been completely erased through forgiveness! It is God's desire that you be an imitator of Him and learn to forgive as He forgives. Because of God's unfailing love for you, when He forgives, He removes your sins as far from you as the east is from the west, and He remembers them no more. Your debt is paid in full through the grace of His blood (Psalm 103:12; Hebrews 8:12).

Forgive through God's grace, and release it

through God's power!

Make allowance for each other's faults, and forgive

anyone who offends you. Remember, the Lord

forgave you, so you must forgive others.

(Colossians 3:13 NLT)

Today's Declaration:

I will forgive quickly and completely, and let it go!

Pearl 34
Be Strong and Courageous

The act of being strong and courageous is not what you do when you are feeling confident and empowered; true strength and courage are manifested when you respond with power and bravery, even in the face of fear and intimidation. You tackle the challenge in the midst of your insecurities realizing that it is not about what you feel that gives you the tenacity you need to conquer the challenge, it is who and what you know that empowers you to overcome! You have confident assurance that through God's strength, you can do anything and that His greatness within you far supersedes any power that could ever come against you! So gird up your strength, manifest your courage, and know He has already made you an overcomer!

Have I not commanded you? Be strong and of good courage; do not be afraid, nor be dismayed, for the Lord your God is with you wherever you go.

(Joshua 1:9 NKJV)

Today's Declaration:

I will not be afraid; God is with me!

Pearl 35
Reappoint Your
Disappointments

Do you really believe with full assurance that God always has your best interest at heart and that He has the perfect plan for your life? Sometimes when your plans for your life do not succeed, you feel disappointed, confused or even upset because you do not understand why things did not turn out the way you hoped they would. Reappoint your disappointments by using them not as weights that foster heaviness and mental anguish, but as stepping stones that push you to your next level of faith and glory! Completely submerge your thoughts, emotions, and spirit in the uplifting and refreshing truth. Even when you do not understand, God is still in control, and He is directing your steps day by day to greater destiny!

If you trust God with your life and do not depend

on the frailty of your human understanding, He

will lead you to an expected end that far outweighs

what you could ever think or imagine!

The Lord directs our steps, so why try to

understand everything along the way?

(Proverbs 20:24 NLT)

Today's Declaration:

I will trust God's plans for my life!

Pearl 36
Come Out of the Pit

Have you ever felt like you were in a pit that you just could not get out of by yourself? Pits are often dark, lonely, and cold, and they breed feelings of hopelessness. When you look around, it seems that there is no way out. The devil enjoys seeing believers of God in the pit - the pit of despair, depression, frustration, worry, anger, bitterness, fear, sin, lack and the list goes on. But even in a pit, there is a way out. Just look up! At the top of that dark pit is a way of escape already prepared so God can rescue and deliver you! All hope is not lost. You will not be in this tight spot always, and you are not alone. God is with you even in the pit, and He will pull you up and out, if you cry out to

Him in your distress. God is your great deliverer! It is time for you to come out - out of the pit!

I waited patiently for the Lord; and He inclined to me, and heard my cry. He also brought me up out of a horrible pit, out of the miry clay, and set my feet upon a rock, and established my steps.

(Psalm 40:1-2 NKJV)

Today's Declaration:

No more "pit stops" for me; I am free!

Pearl 37
God's Everlasting Love

God's love for you never changes, and it never fails.

God never falls out of love with you. His love is

sure, unfailing, unconditional, and proven. He

sacrificed His son Jesus' life for you while you were

yet in sin. He made ways for you even when you

were dirty with sin and too ashamed to ask Him to

move on your behalf. He pulled you out of dark

places that you felt stuck. What a loving God! God

doesn't love you because of what you do or don't

do. He loves you simply because He is love and

because you are His beloved child. As His children,

we are so undeserving and sometimes so

ungrateful, but God still will not let anything

separate you from His love! Can you take a

moment right now and celebrate God's

unconditional and unfailing love for you?

Give thanks to the God of heaven, for His steadfast

love endures forever. (Psalm 136:26 ESV)

Today's Declaration:

I am grateful for God's everlasting love for me!

Pearl 38
Enter God's Rest

Busy schedules. Scattered thoughts. Anxieties, worries, and frustrations. Each of these can cause restlessness in your mind, emotions, and bodies. But, there is a supernatural rest that God has made available to all who are willing to exchange their worries and unrest for His serenity. God's rest is peace in the midst of confusion. God's rest is joy in the face of tribulation. God's rest is refreshment in His presence. God's rest is knowing the truth that everything is going to be alright. Let God lead you beside still waters and give you rest. Rest your mind. Rest your body. Rest your spirit. Rest your emotions. Lay all your burdens down at God's feet, and just rest in Him.

Then Jesus said, "Come to me, all of you who are weary and carry heavy burdens, and I will give you rest. (Matthew 11:28 NLT)

Today's Declaration:

I will rest in God!

Pearl 39
Imitators of Christ

Character. Integrity. Morality. Truth. Consistency. Righteousness. Each of these are characteristics that should be reflected in your daily life as a believer in Jesus Christ. Believers and even non-believers should be able to mark the path of a believer and follow Him or her as they follow Christ (Phil. 3:17). But, does your lifestyle attract or repel others from knowing the Christ you confess lives within you? You should live in such a way that you are not stumbling blocks to the development of another's faith, spiritual walk or relationship with God. Your lifestyle should not be hypocritical to your confession. You have the awesome responsibility to reflect the essence of Christ to those who are lost and to be an example to those striving to live a life pleasing to God. The question each of us as believers must ask ourselves daily is, "How am I living?"

Decide instead to live in such a way that you will

not cause another believer to stumble and fall.

(Romans 14:13b NLT)

Today's Declaration:

I will walk as an imitator of Christ that others may

imitate me!

Pearl 40
Even More

The Lord spoke these words to my spirit in a
dream one evening and impressed within me to
declare it over the lives of those who would receive
it by faith - even more! You are already blessed,
but you are about to experience an outburst of
even more blessings in your life. Even more power
and anointing; even more favor and glory; even
more faith and strength; even more revelation and
knowledge; and even more joy and peace! More
creativity, innovation, and prosperity! Your cup is
getting ready to overflow! But remember: what is in
your cup is designed to be a blessing to you, and
the overflow is given to you to be a blessing to
others. Get ready for increase, overflow, and even

more in every area of your life! It is so, in Jesus'
Name!

The Lord shall increase you more and more, you

and your children. (Psalm 115:14 KJV)

Today's Declaration:

I receive the increase and abundance of blessings

that are coming to me!

Pearl 41
Teach Me

Teach me how to live, O Lord! Teach me how to abandon what is wrong and embrace what is right. Teach me how to crucify my flesh and renew my mind. Teach me how to discern darkness from light. Teach me how to steward my earthly responsibilities and balance my Kingdom assignments with excellence and truth. Teach me how to be thankful, even when my heart is overwhelmed; teach me how to find peace, joy, and contentment in the simple things of life. Teach me how to overcome fear with faith and weakness with Your power. Teach me how to search for You in every moment and in every situation. Teach me how to submit myself to You and follow You as You lead me. Teach me how to love You fervently and serve You wholeheartedly. Teach me. I want to live better. I want to live right. I want to live for You - completely. Teach me how to live, O Lord!

Teach me how to live, O LORD. Lead me along the right path... (Psalm 27:11a NLT)

Today's Declaration:

I submit my life to you, O Lord; teach me!

Pearl 42
Abound in Hope

Hope has been defined as a strong feeling of trust
and expectation that a certain thing is going to
happen. When you choose to hope in God and in
the good plans He has for your life, regardless of
negative circumstances, it dispels the dark clouds
of despair, doubt, fear, and hopelessness that
drain your joy and peace. When Abraham was
waiting for God's promise to manifest that he
would be the father of many nations, the Bible
says that even when there was no reason for hope,
Abraham kept hoping - believing that God would
do just what He said until the promise was fulfilled.
Those who put their hope in God will not be
disappointed! May God, who is the Hope of Glory,
birth fresh hope within you today that will bring

overwhelming peace and joy to your heart and mind!

Now the God of hope fill you with all joy and peace in believing, that ye may abound in hope, through the power of the Holy Ghost. (Romans 15:3 KJV)

Today's Declaration:

My heart is full of hope in God, and it will not be disappointed!

Pearl 43
Pruning for Growth

It is hard to press towards the new when you keep looking back at what you have lost. Release people, things, and personal attitudes God has cut from your life as part of your pruning process. They were stunting your growth in many areas and were hindering you from being progressively and abundantly fruitful and productive. Stay intently focused on the mark of the higher calling that God has set before you, with no looking back, and discover the greater works God will perform through you. If you allow God to cut off unproductive things in your life, your life will blossom in ways you never imagined. Submit yourself to the pruning process, and let God, the Divine Gardener, complete His work in you!

He cuts off every branch in me that bears no fruit,

while every branch that does bear fruit He prunes

so that it will be even more fruitful. (John 15:2 NIV)

Today's Declaration:

Prune me that I may bear more fruit and grow in

You, O God!

Pearl 44
Smooth Sailing

Don't allow the enemy, the devil, to make you think

your way is going to be difficult and hard. Cast down

demeaning thoughts that cause you to think

negatively, pessimistically or the worst about the path

God is allowing you to take. Instead, fix your thoughts

on the Word of God that brings direction, life, and

peace. Even when you experience hardship, the love

and comfort He provides for you makes the hardship

easier to bear. The way of the transgressor is hard, but

God watches over the path of the righteous to ensure

victory every time (Prov. 13:15; Psalm 34:19). This truly

is your time for divine manifestation and fulfillment of

God's promises. The worst is behind you, and the rest

is smooth sailing. God has gone before you and made

the crooked places straight!

But for those who are righteous, the way is not steep and rough. You are a God who does what is right, and you smooth out the path ahead of them.

(Isaiah 26:7 NLT)

Today's Declaration:

God is smoothing the path for me!

Pearl 45
The Power to Overcome

In this season of elevation and fulfillment of God's promises in your life, don't allow fear or intimidation to cause you to cower back from the divine opportunities, assignments, and open doors God will set before you. Your first reaction will be to stay in your comfort zone because you will feel the task God is calling you to is too great for you; but, be encouraged. You are well-equipped to overcome the task set before you! God is working in you, and He is giving you the desire to do His will and to come up higher and accept the challenge of a new level and a new assignment in Him. Depend on God's strength, be bold and courageous, and do what pleases Him. You will succeed and triumph every time! Failure is not an option for you!

Let us go up at once, and possess it; for we are well

able to overcome it. (Numbers13:30b KJV)

Today's Declaration:

I will overcome everything that I am facing through

the power of Jesus Christ!

Pearl 46
Trust God with Your Life

Do you trust God with your life - with every detail of it? You may have answered "Yes," but how often do you wholeheartedly seek the Lord for His guidance, wisdom, and instruction on what to do? How often do you ask Him to do things in your life and then actually wait patiently for Him to show you the way, instead of just acting? God loves you so much! He does not just desire *good* for you; He desires the *best* for you! He wants you to seek Him, receive and follow His words that reveal His perfect plan, and trust Him with everything you are, everything you have, and with everything you are doing. Do not forfeit receiving divine clarity which reveals God's best for you because of fear and control that prevents you from fully trusting Him with every detail of your life. Trust God with your life, and experience God's bestin every area!

Let the morning bring me word of your unfailing love, for I have put my trust in you. Show me the way I should go, for to you I entrust my life. (Psalm 143:8 NIV)

Today's Declaration:

I trust God with every detail of my life!

Pearl 47
Change the Atmosphere

Can God trust you to be light and salt in a spiritually dark and flavorless world? In order to reflect true Christianity, you must represent members of the Kingdom who live by the truth of God's Word and who joyously express that living for Christ is not burdensome. It is time for believers to come forth and shine in dark places and change bland atmospheres where God is not being represented so that hearts can be transformed! Many Christians are tempted to stay within the social confines of only others carrying light and salt. Light does not need more light; but, darkness craves it. Seasoned environments do not need more flavor, but flavorless ones are desperate for it. What atmosphere or individual life has been changed because of the light and salt of Christ you are carrying? Resolve to be salt and light and to change lives through them!

You are the salt of the earth; but if the salt loses its flavor, how shall it be seasoned? You are the light of the world. A city that is set on a hill cannot be hidden. (Matthew 5:13a-14 NKJV).

Today's Declaration:

I am an atmosphere changer!

Pearl 48
Character Test

As you press toward the fulfillment of God's promises for your life, God tests and proves you to determine if you are ready to handle the promises with good character and integrity. How can God trust you with the promise, if your character is not intact to maintain it? Character refers to our moral or ethical quality. In simpler terms, it has been said that character is doing the right thing when no one is looking. Joseph endured and passed the character tests on his way to the fulfillment of God's promise for his life. He could have slept with Potiphar's wife, but he said "No!" He could have hated his brothers, but he forgave them. He could have grown bitter toward God because of his continual hardships and trials, but he loved and trusted Him even more. In the end, God trusted

Joseph with the promise of promotion because he showed his Godly character though trials. Is your character intact to receive and maintain the promise?

Until the time came to fulfill his dreams, the LORD tested Joseph's character. (Psalm 105:19 NLT)

Today's Declaration:

I will live with good character so that God can trust me with the promise!

Pearl 49
Walk in Peace

Don't allow anything or anyone to steal your peace.
Peace of the heart and mind is a gift and promise
of God to those who love Him. The cares of this
world and the devil's agents will attempt to destroy
our peace by causing anxiety and fear and by
sowing negativity and doubts through their words
and deeds. However, learn to guard your peace by
standing steadfastly on the promises of God. Allow
nothing to shake your peace! Trials and spiritual
attacks of the devil only last for a short time, but
God's gifts and promises are eternal. Your peace is
designed by God to outlast and to overcome any
force that tries to come against it. May you walk in
God's peace in every situation and at all times by
bringing to your remembrance God's promises

concerning what you are going through. Let God's peace guard your heart and mind through it all!

I will listen to what God the LORD says; He promises peace to His people, His faithful servants.

(Psalm 85:8a NIV)

Today's Declaration:

I will listen to God and walk in His peace in every situation!

Pearl 50
Focus on Your Dreams

Focus your thoughts, motivations, energies, and plans on only divinely-given dreams. Your dream will only be realized through the energy you put into it! So, don't busy yourself with activities that drain your energy and creative abilities so that you have very little left to accomplish *your* dreams. The oil God has given you to complete your divine assignment is precious and costly and should flow toward the purpose God intends. Allow God, the One who knows the plans He has for you, to lead you along the paths to the fulfillment of your dreams. He has handcrafted your expected end. If you seek God's wisdom in all you do, He will reveal to you whether an activity is profitable or not for you. Listen closely and intently as He reveals His will to you. Profitless activities are destiny detours

that can hinder your focus and deter you from

your Godly destination. Busy yourself on what

matters most, and keep your focus!

Too much activity gives you restless dreams.

(Ecclesiastes 5:3a NLT)

Today's Declaration:

Help me, Lord, to avoid distractions and to focus

intently on Your divine purpose for my life!

Pearl 51
Return to God

Have you ever gone astray even after confessing

Jesus as your Lord and Savior? With great shame

and distress, you may have found that trying to

chart your path and live according to your foolish

wisdom and fleshly desires only lead to

discontentment and lack of fulfillment. During

these times of backsliding and rebellion from God,

you may have tried to find direction from all of the

wrong sources and love in all of the wrong places.

You may have neglected the realization that the

only one who can guide you into His truth and

satisfy your heart with His unfailing love is God

Himself. He quenches the thirst and longing of

your heart like no one and nothing else can. Since

you serve such a loving God, even after you have

tried walking away from Him to pursue avenues in life that reap no holy benefits, God is still seeking and calling for you to come back to Him with open arms. What an amazingly loving God we serve! Will you heed His call?

But you have lived as a prostitute with many lovers – would you now return to me? declares the LORD.

(Jeremiah 3:1b NIV)

Today's Declaration:

I will repent of my wrong, return to my God, and receive His amazing love!

Pearl 52
Live a Content Life

It is God's desire for His children to live in contentment and satisfaction with the blessings He has provided for us to enjoy! The enemy oftentimes tries to steal your joy through feelings of discontentment enticing you to look at what you do not have rather than focusing on the wealth of blessings that God manifests daily in your life. The Lord provides what you need because of His faithfulness and love for you, and He gives you the desires of your heart when you delight yourself in Him. If there is something that you desire that has not been granted, rely on the sovereignty of God. He will provide only what is right and good for you; those things that in His infinite wisdom He deems you are able and ready to handle. Rejoice in your abundance of blessings, and be careful to never minimize God's goodness.

Enjoy what you have rather than desiring what you don't have. (Ecclesiastes 6:9a NLT)

Today's Declaration:

I will no longer focus on what I do not have but appreciate every blessing God has provided for me!

Pearl 53
Joy in the Rain

On the day of my oldest son's 10th birthday party, he woke up excited and full of anticipation about the day's activities, until he heard the heavy downpour of rain outside. Immediately, his heart began to sink, and his mind was flooded with discouraging thoughts which turned his countenance very sad. His father and I began to encourage him to shift his attention to the blessings that rain brings and to not let the rain steal his joy. How often do you allow your excitement and anticipation for things you once trusted God to fulfill to wane away by the rains of life? Do you not realize that God allows rain in your life to cleanse you, to strengthen you, and to develop greater fruit within you? Rain in your life does not cancel God's plans for you! We have to remind ourselves, when we are tempted to sink into puddles of despair, that there is still much to celebrate and to be thankful for even in the midst of the rain!

Why are you cast down, O my soul? And why are you disquieted within me? Hope in God; for I shall yet praise Him, the help of my countenance and my God. (Psalm 42:11NKJV)

Today's Declaration:

I will not let the rains of life destroy my joy because my hope is in God!

Pearl 54
Work the Works

Responsibility, accountability, dedication, and commitment are four integral attributes that are diminishing in society - even among believers. If God has given you an assignment, His desire is for you to serve and to work wholeheartedly, steadfastly, and with a spirit of excellence through the strength and wisdom that He provides. God detests laziness and indifference concerning the use of the gifts, talents, and abilities He has given you. He describes it as wickedness and sin when you do not use them wisely. To have been given an assignment to do and not do it is laziness, and to know what is right to do and not do it is sin (Matt. 25, James 4). May you never be lacking in zeal, but keep your spiritual fervor while you serve God and others. May you never neglect the gifts and abilities within you that God has graced you with. It is such a blessing and a privilege to be used by God, and He depends on gifted and called people like you to be good stewards of the work assigned to your life to help change the lives of others. So, may you work the work!

Don't try to avoid doing your duty.

(Ecclesiastes 8:3a NLT)

Today's Declaration:

I will work the works that my God has given me to do with my whole heart!

Pearl 55
Search My Heart

How often do you ask the Lord to search your heart? This should be a daily prayer for the believer. In the midst of your daily interactions with people and being faced with daily challenges and disappointments, you may become offended, hurt, angry or bitter. Your heart can become contaminated and hardened toward people and even toward God. The longer those contaminants stay there, the dirtier your heart can become. Oftentimes, it is easy to pack those emotions in a deep place within your heart and keep going. But the remedy to having a clean heart is crying out to God daily to search your heart, to point out any wickedness, that He may show you the right way to think, feel, and act in your current situation. Will you allow the Lord to search your heart today?

Search me, O God, and know my heart: try me, and know my thoughts: and see if there be any wicked way in me, and lead me in the way everlasting.

(Psalm 139:23-24 KJV)

Today's Declaration:

Search me, cleanse me, and lead me, O God!

Pearl 56
Trust in God

Trust in God. Trust in the One who created you.
Trust in the One who knew your purpose even
before the world began. Trust in the One who
cannot lie. Trust in the One who will never leave
you. Trust in the One who rules and reigns over
everyone and everything. Trust in the One who
orders your steps and moves your stumbling
blocks. Trust in the One who will not let your foot
slip. Trust in the One who overcame the world and
destroyed the works of the devil to give you the
victory. Trust in the One who knows your needs
even before you ask. Trust in the One who has
nothing but good things planned for you. Trust
God with all your needs, all your desires, and all
your plans, and He will take care of you according

to His divine plan and divine timing. Just trust Him!

Trust in the Lord with all your heart; do not depend on your own understanding. Seek his will in all you do, and he will show you which path to take.

(Prov. 3:5-6 NLT)

Today's Declaration:

My whole heart will trust in You, O God!

Pearl 57
Receive Wise Counsel

Who do you receive counsel and advice from?

Whose guidance and criticisms affect you the most

- those of the wise or those of the foolish? Your

answers to these questions may provide profound

clarity as to why you are excelling and growing by

leaps and bounds or why you feel stagnant,

unproductive or unfulfilled. The company you keep

and those you receive counsel from can either

propel you to your destiny or extinguish the desire

and drive within you to excel. You become the

company that you keep. God warns the believer

not to receive counsel from the ungodly if we want

to flourish and be productive. It is iron that

sharpens iron. Sometimes, you may think that

your way is right in your own eyes, until the

counsel of the wise reveals the error of your way and enlightens your understanding. This may sometimes come in the form of constructive criticism, or a rebuke offered in love that challenges the futility of your thinking. In the end, if you heed sound wisdom, it will bring life to your soul and breed great success!

Better to be criticized by a wise person than to be praised by a fool. (Ecclesiastes 7:5 NLT)

Today's Declaration:

Help me to seek wise counsel and heed wise counsel!

Pearl 58
Submit Your Plans

As a believer, your life is not your own. God has divinely planned a course for your life that, if fully obeyed and followed, will yield a path of abundant blessings and perfect peace. But you must keep your spiritual eyes on God and your spiritual ears attuned to His voice and instructions. You must be careful to submit your will to His and not try to chart your own path without His leading. Human wisdom is foolishness to God, and even the way that you think is right may lead to utter destruction without God's guidance. Listen to the voice of God - that still small voice of the Holy Spirit within you - that leads and guides you day by day. Allow the Word of God to guide your footsteps. Submit your plans to God's plans that promise to produce good, and not evil in your life, and give up trying to plan your own course. God in His sovereignty had every day of your life planned out long before you were born and the course He destined for you to take before the world began. Quiet your soul, and trust His plan!

I know, LORD, that our lives are not our own. We are not able to plan our own course.

(Jeremiah 10:23 NLT)

Today's Declaration:

I completely submit to you, O God, and exchange my plan for Your plan for my life!

Pearl 59
Arise and Shine

What is asleep within you that needs to be awakened and revealed in the earth through the reviving power and light of Jesus Christ? What divine assignment, gift, calling, passion, vision, or dream have you laid to rest or buried within your heart due to fear, circumstances, insecurities, laziness or lack of zeal to pursue what God revealed to you? Now is the time! Now is the time that God is calling for you to awaken from your spiritual slumber and begin seeking His face, discovering His will, and following His plan for your life like never before. When you seek God with your whole heart, God will revive you through His righteousness and bring you forth into the light of His glory! God is urgently calling for His children to arise and shine because the light of His glory has come to bring forth revival in you (Isaiah 60:1) He is reviving those things that have been lying dormant within you; things that have been designed to change the course of your life and empower the lives of others. Are you ready to be revived?

Therefore he says, Awake you that sleep, and arise from the dead, and Christ shall give you light. (Ephesians 5:14 NKJV)

Today's Declaration:

May I awaken from spiritual slumber, and revive the power lying dormant with me!

Pearl 60
Teach Me Your Will

What is the will of the Lord for my life? This question is often asked by believers. God's will is often revealed when you have reached a point of complete submission and surrender to Him and when your heart is willing to offer Him an unrestricted "Yes!" For many of us, it is difficult to release our locus of control or will to God's will and divine control because we are so engrossed in our own plans and desires. It is only when you lose your life for Christ's sake that you find your true purpose and discover His will (Matt. 16:25). God's ways and thoughts are so much higher than yours concerning His plans for your life. So, you must depend on His infinite wisdom, not the futility of your own wisdom, which yields fruitlessness. God's will is greater than yours, and it will produce more in your life than you can ever imagine. Discover what the will of the Lord is for your life, and pursue it with everything you've got!

Therefore do not be unwise, but understanding what the will of the Lord is. (Ephesians 5:17 KJV)

Today's Declaration:

Lord, give me the wisdom to discover your will and the heart of discipline to obey it!

My prayer for every reader of *Pearls for Everyday Life* is that you will walk in the beauty of God's holiness; be filled with unspeakable joy and God's glory; shine with the brightness of hope that only God can give; embrace the unconditional love of God; and share God's love with others. I pray that God adorns you with grace and favor that surpasses anything your mind could think. I pray that your trust in God and His Word will never be shaken, as you continue to meditate on and declare His truth. I declare that the fullness of your destiny *will* manifest with good fruit in its due season. May grace and peace be multiplied to you in the knowledge of God and of Jesus our Lord, as His divine power has given to us all things that pertain to life and godliness, through the knowledge of Him who called us by glory and virtue (II Peter 1:2-3). Amen.

Blessings and Love,

DR. FELISHA FORD

www.drfelishaford.com

Made in United States
Orlando, FL
13 May 2023